Praise from diverse sources for _Embracing Fear_

**A new book about a universal and important subject
by Thom Rutledge
with a Foreword by Oriah Mountain Dreamer**

Take a wonderful journey through and beyond your fear with Thom. You'll enjoy your time with him and learn something practical and valuable about one of our greatest enemies in life—all the boogeymen in our heads.

—Melody Beattie
Author of _Choices_ and _Codependent No More_

Embracing Fear _is an insightful, moving and gracious book. Thom Rutledge understands that fear, like self-consciousness, is part of what it means to be human, so he engages it creatively as a force in life. Reading this book was for me a deeply enriching experience._

—John Shelby Spong
Author of _A New Christianity for a New World_

Thom Rutledge has written a clear guide that shows how to turn fear into a powerful resource in our lives. He draws on his expertise and life experience to help us avoid the destructive consequences of anxiety and unwarranted fear while finding the valuable lessons true fear holds for each of us. Readers will live life a bit more fully with each chapter.

—Gavin de Becker
Author of _The Gift of Fear_ and _Fear Less_

Embracing Fear offers tools and encouragement to help us face, understand and learn from the walls of fear that keep us from moving forward in our lives.

—Debbie Ford
Author of *Secret of the Shadow*

Thom's writing is not only insightful and honest, it is useful for all of us longing, learning and sometimes struggling to lead ordinary human lives, consciously. I use Thom's insights and meditations in my own quest for self-knowledge and in my work with others.

—Oriah Mountain Dreamer
Author of *The Invitation* and *The Dance*

Embracing Fear is a book for our times.

Fear lives in all of us. It haunts us day and night and prevents us from living to our potential. Whether we are afraid of the dark, being alone, rejection, failure, commitment, public speaking, flying, or impending death, these fears are motivating factors in all aspects of our lives. In *Embracing Fear* psychotherapist Thom Rutledge combines compelling anecdotes from his practice and his own experience of addiction and depression with exercises and empowering tools. Rutledge uses the acronym F-E-A-R as a model to guide readers through the process. Instead of running, repressing or ignoring the voices of panic and dread, we learn that it is only through **F**acing, **E**xploring, **A**ccepting, and **R**esponding consciously to fear that we become free from its paralyzing grip. Rutledge says, "Always move toward your demons; they take their power from your retreat."

With over 20 years experience as a psychotherapist, Thom Rutledge is an accomplished author and popular keynote speaker. For more information about Mr. Rutledge and his book, *Embracing Fear*, visit http://www.thomrutledge.com, or e-mail thomrutledge@earthlink.net.

Nutshell Essays

Nutshell Essays

◆

52 Brief Lessons for Big Change

Wisdom, humor & inspiration from the author of
Embracing Fear

Thom Rutledge

iUniverse, Inc.
New York Lincoln Shanghai

Nutshell Essays
52 Brief Lessons for Big Change

iUniverse, Inc.

For information address:
iUniverse, Inc.
2021 Pine Lake Road, Suite 100
Lincoln, NE 68512
www.iuniverse.com

Thom Rutledge Publishing
331 22nd Avenue North, Suite One
Nashville, Tennessee 37203
(615) 327-3423
thomrutledge@earthlink.net

ISBN: 0-595-28005-6 (pbk)
ISBN: 0-595-74887-2 (cloth)

Printed in the United States of America

For the amazing women of Monday night.

Contents

Introduction

✦

The Birth of E-minders

In the summer of 2000 I began work on a new book to be published by Harper-SanFrancisco, thanks to the helping hand of a friend whom I had never met.

HarperSanFrancisco had published Oriah Mountain Dreamer's best selling book, *The Invitation*, earlier that year, and in response to that amazing book I had contacted Oriah. Because of our correspondence and her beginning to use a couple of exercises from one of my previous books in her workshops, Oriah was kind enough to recommend me to her literary agent, Joseph Durepos. Joe called me one late afternoon with an idea for a new book to be based on a visualization I had written called The Wall. In our efforts to develop a proposal for a book about resistance to change (aka: The Wall), we eventually came to understand that what we were really talking about was how people relate to fear. So with the generous help of Oriah Mountain Dreamer, whom I still have never met in person, and my new literary agent, Joe Durepos, I was given the opportunity to write *Embracing Fear & Finding the Courage to Live Your Life*.

Knowing that I would soon have a book published by a major publisher, I decided it was time to reach a broader audience for my writing. Since I had finally been introduced to the wonderful world of computers (I had been very slow in coming around, having such affection for my still-modern-in-my-eyes IBM Selectric typewriter), I hit upon the idea of writing a weekly e-mail feature to be sent out to people who would subscribe via my new web site. On September 11, 2000—exactly one year before the terrorist attacks in New York, Pennsylvania and Washington D.C.—I wrote and sent out the first issue of "E-Minders for the Therapeutically Forgetful." (The title was inspired by something I once heard someone say about the human condition: it is a condition of chronic forgetfulness.)

I was pleasantly surprised with a rapidly growing subscriber list due in large part to word of mouth from my very supportive readers, and within a few months realized that I might well be on my way to a collection of short essays that could become another book. In the last several months, having received an increasing number of requests for back issues of E-minders, I have realized the time is right to create a couple of volumes of my nutshell essays. And what better format for my E-minders than an e-book? And so here you have *Nutshell Essays*.

The essays that follow remain in the order in which they were published as E-minders. Other than the few that are written specifically for holidays, one written for April Fool's Day, and the E-minders written in response to the 9-11-01 tragedy (one of which was written by my assistant because I just couldn't pull it off), there is no particular plan for the sequence in this book. There are a few that are written as series (parts 1, 2, 3, etc), but otherwise each entry is written to stand completely on its own.

I am currently at work on some other projects that I hope will see the light of day in the publishing world in the next couple of years, and I am seeking as much publicity for *Embracing Fear* as possible. (All help is welcome in that regard.) In the meantime, I will continue to turn out my weekly E-minders, so if you are not already on the subscriber list and want to be, let me know by e-mailing thomrutledge@earthlink.net with "subscribe" in the subject line.

I am grateful to all of my readers for such enthusiastic and active support through the years.

Of course I could not do any of this without the clients who trust me enough to let me into their lives. Also I want to thank Dede Beasley, Joe Durepos, Oriah Mountain Dreamer, Gideon Weil, Liz Winer, Margery Buchanan, Jennifer Schaefer, Jana Stanfield, Debi Smith and Scott Weiss for their moral support and practical assistance every step of the way.

Now I hope that you will enjoy and benefit from my nutshell essays. If you do, please help me tell the rest of the world. If you happen to be Oprah's best friend, please don't hesitate to put in a good word for me.

Thanks.

Thom Rutledge
May 2003

1

Forget about control.

One of the keys to success is accepting full responsibility for yourself. Accepting this responsibility, contrary to popular belief, has nothing to do with being "in control." There is a major distinction to be made between being "in control" and accepting the responsibility of being "in charge" of your life. Simply put: You have nothing to say about the cards dealt you, but everything to say about how you will play those cards.

A victim will blame the dealer of the cards, or blame the person who taught him how to play cards, or maybe even the cards themselves. A victim may even take refuge in blaming himself, not understanding that there is an important difference between "self-blame," and "accepting responsibility."

Victimization is a state of mind in which you believe that how you are doing in any particular moment is determined more by the circumstances beyond your control than by how you choose to respond to those circumstances. A non-victim knows that the key is in our ability to respond—get it: response-ability.

To accept full responsibility for yourself, you must renounce victimization.

In a Nutshell

*Being a victim is an
indulgence we cannot afford.*

*Be "in charge," but forget
about being "in control."*

2

Perfectionism is about self-criticism, not about success.

Aerfectionist is not someone who does things perfectly; a perfectionist is someone who believes he or she is supposed to do things perfectly. Perfectionism is a condition of constant pain, and self-absorption. Contrary to popular opinion, striving for perfection is not productive; it is destructive—at its worst, suicidal. By constantly expecting the impossible of yourself (perfection), you set yourself up to fail—over and over again.

To be successful you must become both optimistic and realistic. This requires that you come to terms with your own human imperfection. To pretend that your very real human flaws do not exist is certain self-sabotage, as is thinking of yourself as nothing but flaws.

In your efforts (imperfect efforts) to recognize that perfection is not even one of your choices, you will come face to face with perfectionism's energy source: self-criticism. You must learn to identify and reject the highly negative-biased view associated with your self-critical thinking. In other words, since we don't know how to get rid of self-critical thinking, you will need to learn to disagree with your own negative views of yourself. Claim the right to disagree with yourself—and exercise that right often.

Instead of seeking perfection, try this: Do the very best you can. Challenge yourself to stretch beyond your current level of competence, but do not expect the impossible—do not expect perfection. Remember this simple plan: When you fall, get up. When you forget, remember. Expect to fall and forget frequently.

In a Nutshell

Perfectionism is a state of
constant self-victimization.

2

3

There is such a thing as too much humble pie.

Everyone has known someone who apologizes incessantly. "I'm sorry about this, I'm sorry about that, I'm sorry for everything, even if I had nothing to do with it." These people have eaten one too many slices of humble pie. And if you confront them with how irritating their constant apologizing is, what do they instantly do? Apologize, of course.

Don't be one of these people, and if you have been, for goodness sake, don't apologize for it.

Too much humble pie (aka: rock bottom self-esteem) is a strange and interesting thing. To think that things are not going well in your life because you are a worthless piece of crap will not help you to accept responsibility for yourself. Quite the opposite: hiding behind self-blame, and drowning in the resulting shame is one of the most efficient—not to mention prevalent—ways to avoid personal responsibility. This is the self-absorbed state of "Negative Arrogance." I once heard this state of mind described as a belief that says, "I am the piece of crap that the world revolves around." When I first heard that, it sounded waaaaay too familiar to me; that was the day I made a commitment to stop living my life as a victim. And I work to live up to that commitment one day at a time.

In a Nutshell

*Victimization is a
self-fulfilling prophecy,
and self-condemnation
has nothing to do with
being a responsible person.*

4

Beware of the "value split."

We each have two distinct value systems. One is the value system we express, and the other is the value system we demonstrate through our behavior. On a daily basis we strive to bring these two value systems as close to alignment as possible—or we invest our energy in trying not to recognize the discrepancy between the two. (What we don't acknowledge can't hurt us, our misplaced optimism tells us.) I think it is safe to say that most of us do some of both of these.

The experience of addiction provides the most blatant examples of a split between our two value systems. In the final months of my first marriage, had you asked me if I valued my marriage or my drinking more, I would have told you quite sincerely that my marriage was the more important of the two. Everything in my behavior said otherwise. When there is a discrepancy between expressed and demonstrated values, the demonstrated behavior is the credible one.

In our day-to-day lives, however, the challenge of aligning our demonstrated values with our expressed values is usually more complex—or at least it feels that way. I may think something I hear about is a "good cause," but I don't take any action to support it. I may believe that family is more important than work, but choose to put some work considerations first in my life. I may have concerns about how cattle are handled by the beef industry, but enjoy steak on a regular basis. These discrepancies don't make us bad people, but hopefully our increasing awareness of the two distinct value systems will be the pebble in our shoe to keep us awake as we walk the path—motivating us to examine our beliefs, and our choices based on those beliefs, more carefully.

5

Ask yourself good questions.

Y ou cannot create lasting and positive change in your circumstances without changing yourself. No matter how much you know about what needs to change in the people and situations around you, the most powerful way to make things happen is to ask yourself good questions.

Some questions we ask ourselves will only leave us stuck, in that familiar endless cycle—these are questions like "Why can't I ever do anything right?" or "Why am I such an idiot?" Think about it: even if we just slightly change that question to "What can I do today to be less of an idiot?" it becomes a more productive, even though it remains self-abusive. It's a positive step in the right direction. Two of the best questions to ask in any situation are "What am I doing here that is not working?" and "What do I need to be doing instead?"

Practice tuning into your thoughts during times of stress and conflict; listen for the questions you are asking yourself; and change some of the questions to see what will happen.

6

Use compassion and confrontation together.

We live in a society that thinks in extremes—black and white, good and bad, right and wrong. We don't have to look any farther than the current Presidential campaign to be reminded of this. Each candidate takes the position that he is absolutely right, and that his opponent is dead wrong—not a little off, not missing an essential piece—dead wrong. Elections in this country resemble competitive athletic events more than intelligent exchanges of ideas. Go team!

We tend to treat ourselves with the same all or none approach. If I make a mistake, then I am a mistake. If I feel dissatisfied about something in my life, then I am an ungrateful so-and-so. If I fall short of my goal, I am a failure.

This is a highly inefficient way of thinking, wasting no-telling how much of our valuable mental energy (and time) beating ourselves up. This is energy that can be put to much better use when we practice combining self-confrontation with self-compassion. Don't let yourself off the hook, but don't sentence yourself to hard time for a misdemeanor. When you make a mistake, recognize it, correct your error, make the appropriate amends (genuine apology, not shame), pat yourself on the back, and get back in the game. Go team!

In a Nutshell

Self-compassion and
personal responsibility
are two sides of the same coin.

7

Spend your energy wisely.

If mental energy was money, how much cash would you be throwing away on self-doubt and self-condemnation every day? Every week? Every month? Every year? And since mental energy can only be put to effective use in the present moment, how much are you throwing away by being stuck in the past and obsessed with the future?

When I notice that I am wasting my valuable mental energy, I use the following visualization to help me regain my focus:

I imagine myself driving down the road with a briefcase full of cash in the passenger seat. I roll down the window, and begin throwing the cash—by the handfuls—out the window as I continue to drive. This image gets my attention; it gives me a disturbing visual representation of how I am wasting mental energy. The good news is that I am allowed to replenish the briefcase full of money at any time. All I need to do is re-focus my valuable mental energy in the present.

Give it a try. Or create your own visualization to remind you to "pay" attention to this present moment.

<u>In a Nutshell</u>

Mental energy can only be used
in the present moment.
It is worthless anywhere else.

8

Do well even when you feel bad.

Some time ago, I was working with a client who had just begun recovery from alcoholism. As he sat down at the beginning of one of our sessions I asked, "How are you doing?" A simple enough question; a question I have been asking clients for 20 years; nothing fancy or intricately therapeutic about it. But his response taught me (reminded me) of a valuable lesson.

He began his response with a question of his own. "Are you asking me how I am 'doing,' or how I am 'feeling?' Because I am 'doing' very well I think. And I 'feel' like sh—." In fact, he was 'doing' very well: staying sober, going to support meetings, calling his AA sponsor, spending time with his family, and showing up at work every day. But he was not 'feeling' well in ways that are predictable for early addiction recovery: he was experiencing anxiety, confusion, shame, and depression. He was feeling overwhelmed, and due to restless sleep, he was physically tired. He 'felt' bad in these many ways, but he was feeling something else, something directly related to how he was 'doing' well. He felt good about himself. At the end of the day, no matter how bad he might feel, for the first time in a long time, his self-respect was in tact.

I spoke with this client recently, and he reported that he continued to 'do' well, and that he was now also 'feeling' very well. His willingness to persist in taking the right action has paid off, but like most good investments, the pay off was not immediate. I think this is a good reminder for us all.

At the end of the day, as you turn off the light, ask "How did I 'do' today?"

<u>In a Nutshell</u>

*Base your self-esteem
more on how you 'do'
than on how you 'feel.'*

9

Split your personality for better mental health.

Imagine your self-critical thinking (that voice in your head who is never satisfied) as a separate person from yourself. Experience yourself not as the one doing the criticizing, but as the one being criticized. Although this is never much fun (standing the line of self-critical fire), separating from that predictable "Should Monster" in your head will create a place for you to form your own separate opinion.

It takes some time, but with practice you will learn to remain separate from self-critical thought—and ultimately to form your own more realistic, more positive (not to mention more accurate) opinions of yourself.

The bad news is that we don't know how to get rid of the "Should Monster." But here is the really good news: since you can't get rid of him, all you have to do is learn to disagree with him. And even when you are having difficulty disagreeing with him, you can still disobey him. For instance, if your "Should Monster" tells you that you are not smart enough or talented enough to take a particular risk that you want to take, disobey him. Don't let him stop you; do what you want to do. This is a very appropriate application of your rebellious tendencies. And most of us have plenty of those "rebellious tendencies" lying around, and could use a way to put them to productive use.

Since you can't "exorcise" your Should Monster, you must "exercise" your ability to disagree with him. Practice disagreeing with—and disobeying—your "Should Monster" every day.

In a Nutshell

*Always reserve the right
to disagree with yourself.*

10

10

Always work from the inside out.

If you want to insure that you are pursuing a path of personal responsibility that will lead you to the success you seek, keep this slogan in mind: "The first part of any problem that I must solve is that which is between me and me."

To look first at your internal conflict does not mean that you will not have legitimate problems with others—your boss, your friend, your spouse, or your colleague. And this is not meant to encourage the old self-victimizing approach of habitually opting for self-blame. Blame and responsibility are not the same thing anyway.

When you begin by resolving inner conflict, you are simply putting first things first. It's the best starting place; the only starting place if you intend to effect real and lasting change. When you begin problem resolution by looking within your-self first, you are "going with the flow," complying with one of nature's laws: growth moves from the inside out.

Consider a seed. Consider a child. Growth in the literal sense is expansion, and expansion by definition moves from the inside out. Can you imagine drop-ping a pebble in a pool of water, and seeing the resulting ripples move from the outer-most point inward toward the point where the pebble was dropped?

In a Nutshell

The change you seek
always begins with you.

11

See the greater possibilities and move in that direction.

Too often we know much more about what we "don't want" than about what we "do want." If we stop there—aware only of our dissatisfaction—we won't know how to change. Consequently, we are prone to return to the safe haven of the familiar—those old patterns of thinking and behaving that we have already effectively proven to be ineffective. Try this instead: once you determine what you don't want, develop specific goals, and set your sights on those specific goals.

Any motivational speaker will tell you that in order to succeed; you must be open to the positive. Learn to see—and to seek—the greater possibilities. Take the time to develop clear images of your goals. Take the risk to practice expecting positive outcomes. When necessary, make use of a simple slogan heard repeatedly in the program of Alcoholics Anonymous: "Fake it 'til you make it." Look to the past only as long as it takes to learn the lesson. Once you identify what you don't want, put into words, and into a visual image, what you do want. Establish a direction.

Knowing that you want to leave a place (or circumstance) is only the beginning. If I tell you simply that I want to get up from this chair, you won't have very much information about my plans. Do I just need to stand up and stretch my legs before I sit back down and type some more? Do I plan to leave the room? Maybe I intend to leave town. But leave town to go where? Without knowing where I want to go—what I want instead of what I have—I will remain aimless.

The same principles apply to any change that you or I desire. Think about the times when you have known what you didn't want, but were not aware of what you wanted instead—an unsatisfactory relationship or job for instance. What did you do in those circumstances? Did you complain? Did you just build a higher tolerance for your dissatisfaction? Wouldn't it have helped to have some direction?

It has been said that life is a journey, not a destination. I like this one better: "Life is a journey with many destinations." When you decide that a change is needed, have a destination in mind.

12

There is no "right way."

Trust no one who will tell you that they have THE answer, THE way, THE plan, THE diet, THE anything. There are probably as many different approaches to genuine self-improvement as there are people, or at least as many different approaches as there are "self-helpers" (like me) on our soap boxes telling you how to do it.

For instance, when you seek help from a mental health professional, don't forget that you are the customer and the professional is the service provider. Be a good consumer; don't walk in, sit down, and give your power away to someone just because they have a degree or a license or whatever hanging on the wall. And beware of the mental health professional who has forgotten that you are the customer.

A word to the wise: take in information—from professionals and/or others in your support system—as raw material to be processed by your own good judgment. Accept nothing at face value. If an idea, a method, or a technique appears to have value for you, take it off the shelf, hold it in your hands, examine it, try it on, or try it out. Accept it as your own only when you decide.

And when making decisions about what works for you, use the line-item veto. You never have to accept anything all or nothing.

In a Nutshell

Respect others' opinions.
Trust your own good judgment.

13

Know the recipe for motivation.

Motivation doesn't just happen. We have to create it, and maintain it. Here are the necessary ingredients:

Dissatisfaction. Typically, we think of dissatisfaction as a negative thing—to be dissatisfied is to be ungrateful or to be a complainer. Dissatisfaction is not "just complaining," and it is not necessarily an absence of gratitude. Dissatisfaction is the important first ingredient in our recipe for motivation. If we do not experience dissatisfaction, there is no reason to change.

Desire to make a change. It is possible to have a certain level of dissatisfaction and not have much of a desire to change. Anyone who has experienced addiction knows this. It is important that we do not assume that just because we are dissatisfied, we have a sufficient desire to change. Ask yourself, "Do I really want to change this?" and do not proceed until your answer is a determined "Yes."

Belief that change is possible. If we have the first two ingredients, but do not believe that the change desired is possible, we will be stopped dead in your tracks. This is why we all need supportive others in our lives who have already made the changes we desire. If they can do it, so can we.

Willingness to do what it takes. The knowledge that change is possible, even the knowledge of how to make the desired change is not enough. There is still one more essential ingredient in our recipe for motivation. We must become willing to take whatever action is need to accomplish our goal. Willingness to act on our own behalf puts the previous three ingredients into play.

Mix these four ingredients together and you will have motivation. And the next time you are not feeling motivated, use this recipe as a trouble-shooting checklist. Check to see which ingredients are missing.

In a Nutshell

Motivation is not a matter of chance;
it is a matter of choice.

14

Consider a new definition for wisdom.

Someone once described adolescence and early adulthood as the age of "anti-wisdom." Developmentally, it is a time when we are certain of all the answers to life's questions (no matter how insecure we really are) and "adults" who tell us otherwise are imbeciles, idiots and fools. It's been quite a while now, but I remember being there. Do you?

As I have grown older, I have realized that not only do I not have the answers to life's questions; I'm not even sure what the questions are.

Life has consistently presented me with lessons about how much I don't know, and how much I don't control. Strangely, these lessons have been positive, at times even comforting. If I could travel back in time to tell this to my 19 year old self, he would surely laugh in my face. (And then go have a drink.)

Here is my new definition for "wisdom":

"Wisdom is the increasing knowledge of all that I do not know, and all that I do not control."

The two lists have been growing steadily, and I suspect they will continue to do so. Genuine wisdom is a humbling experience.

15

There is a difference between tradition and rigidity.

Even in the midst of family and old friends, you are an adult with the right to think for and decide for yourself. Just because something has been done a certain way for however many years—or generations—doesn't mean it can't change now.

Changing old traditions and/or adding new traditions to your holiday plans does not have to be disrespectful or insensitive. You can stand up "for" yourself, without standing "against" someone else.

You cannot, however, control how others may respond to the new, improved you. And if you rock the family boat this holiday season by taking good care of yourself, remember that as long as you do your part to be honest, fair, and respectful, you are not "abusing" someone else just because they are upset with you. Everyone has a right to their opinion and emotional response. But don't forget: this includes you.

In a Nutshell

Independent thought and action
are essential to our well being.

16

...grant me the courage to change the things I can.

Here's a little something to help us stick with those New Year's Resolutions. Use the 7 checkpoints that follow as daily affirmations, and/or the next time you are feeling stuck, read through them to help you identify problem areas.

The 7 Checkpoints Toward Change

1. I know that the resolution of my problem lies within my reach.

2. The motivation for solving my problem is solely my responsibility.

3. I can only change myself, and I will take action to do so.

4. I will seek and accept support for solving my problem.

5. I will recognize and acknowledge improvement when it occurs.

6. I will use new behavior where familiar behavior has been ineffective.

7. I will do whatever it takes to practice self-compassion all along the way.

17

The key to personal growth is to abstain from victimization.

Personal growth work in its many forms—therapy, support groups, self-help seminars, books, tapes, etc—boils down to this: learning to renounce victimization, and learning to embrace personal responsibility. The simple (but essential) understanding of the difference between a victim and a non-victim is the foundation of this work.

Victims are those who believe that how they are doing is determined primarily by "what happens to them," and consequently that their circumstances must change for them to be free to change. In contrast, non-victims believe that how they are doing is determined by "how they respond" to what happens to them. Non-victims understand that external circumstances are very likely to change in response to the actions they take, but that even when such changes do not occur, their well-being remains self-determined.

As corny as this metaphor is, it is still the best one: If I am not a very good card player, and I sit down to a few games with some excellent card players, I could be dealt the better hands all night long, and I will still lose. The excellent card players know how to respond to the cards they are dealt, while I am predominantly a victim to my cards.

In a Nutshell

*Since you can't control
the cards you will be dealt,
make a decision to become
an excellent card player.*

18

Welcome the "weird."

I am reminded on a regular basis that when we work hard to make changes in our lives (changes in ourselves), achieving our goals will not necessarily feel good initially. I have come to recognize a particular word most people use when their personal growth efforts begin to pay off. The word is "weird." That's right, "weird." Isn't that weird?

When you learn to say no for the first time, when you pay attention to your own needs in a situation, when you start living by decision rather than default, it feels "weird." It's like a new pair of shoes that need to be broken in. The weirdness, the initial discomfort, will pass as you continue to practice the new behaviors and the new ways of thinking.

Later, success will feel like success. But try not to feel too discouraged, because first, it will feel "weird."

<u>In a Nutshell</u>

*Progress does not always
feel like progress.*

19

The key to personal growth is to abstain from victimization.

Personal growth work in its many forms—therapy, support groups, self-help seminars, books, tapes, etc—boils down to this: learning to renounce victimization, and learning to embrace personal responsibility. The simple (but essential) understanding of the difference between a victim and a non-victim is the foundation of this work.

Victims are those who believe that how they are doing is determined primarily by "what happens to them," and consequently that their circumstances must change for them to be free to change. In contrast, non-victims believe that how they are doing is determined by "how they respond" to what happens to them. Non-victims understand that external circumstances are very likely to change in response to the actions they take, but that even when such changes do not occur, their well-being remains self-determined.

As corny as this metaphor is, it is still the best one: If I am not a very good card player, and I sit down to a few games with some excellent card players, I could be dealt the better hands all night long, and I will still lose. The excellent card players know how to respond to the cards they are dealt, while I am predominantly a victim to my cards.

20

Caution: even therapy has side effects.

When we forget that therapy, personal growth seminars, and self-help books are means to an end, we're in trouble. All good things have a downside; psychotherapy and self-help exploration are no exception. Therapy has potential sides effects just like medications. We want to benefit from the good that can be done, but need to be aware of the possibility of counterproductive, even dangerous side effects. Here is a list of at least some potential side effects of psychotherapy.

1. <u>Excessive Analysis</u>: Increasingly needing to understand—and explaining—the meaning of everything.

2. <u>Pathological Fairness</u>: Being so invested in "owning your own stuff," that you can no longer reasonably hold others accountable for their choices.

3. <u>The 50/50 Delusion</u>: Believing that relationship problems have a 50/50 responsibility split always. Never accepting nor assigning full responsibility for a situation.

4. <u>Process Dependency</u>: Believing in the adage, "life is a journey, not a destination," to the point of dropping all expectations of arriving anywhere. Consequently, you don't expect or strive for results; you just focus on one long journey.

5. <u>Therapist Dependency</u>: Consulting your therapist on all matters of importance; or asking yourself in these situations, "What would my therapist think is best?"

6. <u>The New, Improved Blame</u>: Avoiding other people's confrontations of you by saying (or at least thinking), "That's your issue."

7. <u>Hyper-Jargon</u>: Speaking in psychological terms (psycho-babble) to the point where other people don't want to talk to you.

8. <u>The All-Purpose Excuse</u>: using what you have learned about yourself in therapy to justify your less-than-responsible actions—as in, "That's just the way I am; I can't help it."

21

The human condition is one of chronic forgetfulness.

Here are five (5) of the simple truths that consistently recur in my life, both professionally and personally. I offer them here as reminders to you, in hopes that you will return the favor somewhere down the line when I will need reminding.

1. We are multiple, not singular in nature.

    This means that the sooner we accept the reality of "the committee" that works within each of us, the better (more sane) we will feel, and the more effectively we will function in our daily lives. Bottom line: we all talk to ourselves; we just need to get better at it.

2. Every dilemma can be translated into "relationship language."

    Understanding our "relationship to a problem" frees us from "being the problem," and empowers us to change our part of that relationship. Once a dilemma is translated into relationship language, we can choose to stand in the healthy, recovery position, facing the Culprit-de-jour (addiction, depression, self-criticism, eating disorder, etc) saying, "I see you, I hear you, and I disagree with you."

3. Self-compassion and personal responsibility are two sides of the same coin.

    When we suffer with low self-esteem, we are in a self-absorbed state of mind that I call "negative arrogance." (e.g. I am the special piece of crap the world revolves around.) When someone does not pick up after himself (be it socks on the floor or emotional self-care), it eventually becomes difficult to be with that person. Pick up your "emotional socks." Contrary to popular opinion, self-compassion is essential if we plan to accept responsibility for ourselves.

4. <u>Perfection is not a choice for human beings.</u>

    Perfectionism is not positive; it is perpetual self-victimization. The challenge is not to accept that we are a "little short" of being perfect, but that we (human beings) can't even see perfect from where we are standing.

5. <u>No one has the answer for everyone.</u>

    To be mentally, emotionally and spiritually healthy, we must remain independent thinkers. Don't give your power always to anyone, no matter how smart or wise you think they may be. "Respect" other people's opinions, and "trust" your own good judgment.

◆   ◆   ◆

And here is something else worth thinking about: There is an important distinction to be made between self-discipline and self-abuse. Consider two meanings for the word "discipline": 1.) punishment, and 2.) practice. How do you use the word.

22

Good communication is an excellent Valentines Day gift.

What follows are 7 important tools to help build effective communication. As with any tools, the first challenge is to learn how and when to use each tool. (A hammer is very important, but I don't want to use it to repair my eyeglasses.) And keep in mind that this is only a starter set. You will hopefully be adding to this collection of tools for the rest of your life.

The Tools:

1. <u>Take Turns</u>. Two separate agendas can seldom be accomplished at once. Establish some ground rules that will insure that you will take enough time for each of you to talk while the other is really listening.

2. <u>Give Information</u>. State your perceptions and your feelings concisely and respectfully. Avoid "selling your side" as the gospel truth, even when it feels that way to you. To resolve any conflict, room must be made for at least two different perspectives. And remember that emotions are subjective information, not open for debate (i.e. "you shouldn't feel guilty," or "you have no right to be angry").

3. <u>Gather Information</u>. You have a responsibility in communication to do your share of listening, being receptive to what your partner is saying, without immediately judging and categorizing. Ask questions with curiosity, like a good interviewer. And—here comes the radical part—listen to the answers. Too often we ask questions not to gather information, but to make a point.

4. <u>Problem Solve with Benevolence</u>. Be certain to clarify your intention (especially in conflict communication) as seeking a satisfactory outcome for both of you. Find common ground on which to base your communication (i.e.

"We each want to be heard completely and accurately," and/or "We need to make a decision about…") Avoid seeking agreement about perceptions or feelings as a communication goal. There must be room for both of you to win.

5. Future Orient to Problem Solve. Those who forget the past are, in fact, doomed to repeat it. True. But those who won't let go of the past may also be contributing to its repetition. In conflict communication it is best to state complaints about past behaviors clearly and concisely, and then to "future orient." That is, sink most of your energy into describing and/or requesting what you want or need from your partner beginning now. You must be willing to take the chance that your partner wants to and can change along with you. (If you are not able to muster any faith that your partner is willing and/or capable of change, you are probably not working on the most serious problem in your relationship. Get some help.)

6. Take Breaks. Each of you must have the authority to call time out. And each of you must learn to respect time outs when they are called. Call time out when you recognize old, dysfunctional patterns of communication taking over. (They seem to have a life of their own.) When you call time out, it is imperative that you later initiate a time to talk again. Don't just leave it hanging.

7. Backtrack. This is my favorite tool, probably because I have had to use it so often. All progress is not forward. Sometimes the best you can do is stop mid-mistake, apologize and ask for an opportunity to try again ("do-overs" I believe we used to call them). But be careful to not ask for that chance if you do not think you can follow through with some new and improved communication. If you are not ready yet, try apologizing and step back to step 6: take a break.

And remember: practice makes…practice.

In a Nutshell

Without a shared goal,
any attempt at
communication is doomed.

23

Self-respect is the most important respect you can earn.

To earn your own respect, you must live responsibly. To live responsibly, you must identify and clarify your personal value system, and act on a daily basis in accordance with that value system. You will respect yourself to the degree that you do not violate your own value system.

None of us will live in perfect harmony with our personal value systems, not as long as we are human anyway. If you make such perfection a goal, you will be wasting valuable energy that could be put to much better use. Use that energy instead to remain aware of what you value, aware of the choices you make as you walk through your daily life, and aware of the degree of congruence between these two. When you notice that your "behavioral values" are drifting away from your "expressed values," wake yourself up, and return the two to closer alignment.

Just as in a breath-counting meditation, when you lose count, and gently return your undisciplined mind back to "one," it is wise to expect that your behavioral choices will tend to be less disciplined than your expressed personal value system. Condemning yourself for this normal human trait will always be a waste of your time. This is life's meditation, and the point of the meditation is to practice being awake so that you will be living your life by decision rather than by default. Remember: practice makes practice. Perfection will not be attained. Make it your goal to continue this daily practice until you have no breath to count.

Instead of striving for perfection ask yourself, "How can I live this day in a way that even if I were later given the opportunity to change it, I wouldn't want to?"

In a Nutshell

SELF-HELP IN THREE D:
Decision turns
Desperation into
Determination.

24

One breath is better than none.

I am restless by nature. Having made many attempts at establishing a daily practice of meditation, and always feeling like I didn't have time for it, I hit upon the idea of a one-breath meditation. I knew that my "not having time" was just an excuse, although it was an accurate expression of my priorities. The one-breath meditation took away any and all excuses about time. After all, who can claim that they don't have time to take a breath? (Or rather, who can make such a claim with any credibility?)

The One-Breath Meditation:

Before leaving your home each day, sit down in a comfortable position. You don't need a designated place, just sit anywhere comfortable. Keeping you back straight (plain old good posture), slowly take in one full breath. Imagine yourself filling up with clear, clean, fresh energy throughout your whole body.

At the end of the inhale, wait to exhale for about five seconds. Then exhale, releasing your breath slowly, imagining that you are clearing your body and mind of all that is used, stale, or toxic. Just when you believe you have completed the exhale, push a little more air out of your lungs. (You will be surprised how much is left in there.)

Lastly, while you are resuming your normal breathing, remain still for about ten more seconds.

That's all there is to it. It will definitely take you longer to read and think about this E-Minder than it will take you to complete the One-Breath Meditation. I dare you to tell me that you don't have time.

<u>In a Nutshell</u>

The difference between knowledge
and wisdom is experience.

31

25

Take a risk today.

Writing and publishing my first book in 1990 was probably the greatest self-image battle I have ever faced—so far. As long as I postponed writing it, I remained a "potentially" great writer. By actually writing the book, I was trading my safe, secure "potential success" for the real world possibilities of rejection and failure. When the book was complete, my good friend, Evelyn, wrote me this short note:

"Writing is a death defying high wire act, and you have pulled it off."

Evelyn's words marked a turning point on how I perceive myself—not only as a writer, but as a human being. I keep that brief note close by, to remind me—not so much that I have fulfilled a dream, but that I am living in the real world. I took a big risk, my big risk, and it became a right of passage into a strange new world of genuine self-responsibility. I would have never guessed the real world could be so much fun.

As a recovering alcoholic, I learned the value of not taking the insane risks associated with my addiction. But I have also learned that there are sane risks. These are the risks we take in our daily lives to avoid becoming stuck in the quicksand of second-guessing and self-doubt. These are the risks we take when we stand up…and tell our Should Monsters to sit down.

And then there are the bigger risks—like writing my first book; like the work I am doing now on my seventh book. These risks are more than just sane; they are necessary for our sanity.

Have you faced your big risks? Are you facing one now? Life is a death defying high wire act. Are you pulling it off?

<u>In a Nutshell</u>

See clearly.
Make plans.
Take action.
Expect results.

26

Arts and crafts can be helpful.

This is an assignment that my friend and colleague, Trish Sanders, has given her clients from time to time. When her clients are having a difficult time "holding on to their power" in the face of stressful circumstances, Trish suggests they give a little time to creating a design and/or slogan they can draw or write on a T-shirt that can be worn beneath their clothing so that only they know about the special undergarment.

One client, Bess, brought a blank white T-shirt to a therapy session and designed an emblem of a shield. On the shield were depictions of things and ideas that symbolized her personal power, including phrases like…

- I'll choose my own opinions.

- Step back.

- I trust the person beneath this shield.

- Anti-Should Armor

- …and a drawing of herself as a strong, powerful decision-making adult protecting a small child.

Bess wore her "shield" beneath a favorite sweater to a Christmas family reunion. She reported excellent results. "It was like doing a therapy experiment," she told Trish. "I actually had fun."

Try this arts and crafts approach sometime when you can use a strong, tangible reminder of your right and your responsibility to take good care of yourself. You can create your power T-shirt alone, but I think that it is particularly empowering to have a supportive friend or therapist work with you. Somehow the T-shirt is more powerful when someone else knows your secret.

This is a little embarrassing to admit, but sometimes when I am especially nervous about a seminar or speech, I will secretly wear a T-shirt with the Superman emblem on it. And Bess is right: it's kind of fun.

27

Increasing awareness and taking certain actions will result in self-compassion.

The key to making real and lasting change is to focus on one particular relationship that is at the center of each of our lives: the relationship with ourselves—that all important relationship between me and me and between you and you. Unfortunately, many of us are taught to define ourselves only in relationship to others (people, places & things), and we do not have an effective model for developing the self-compassion that not only enables us to feel good about who we are, but also increases effectiveness and productivity in all areas of our lives.

In order to improve our relationship with the Self, there are five steps of awareness and action that must be traversed. (These 5 steps are the original basis for The Self-Forgiveness Handbook) I will present them here in abbreviated form—self-help in a nutshell.

The Five Steps

1. ACKNOWLEDGING THE COMMITTEE. First, we must admit that "I am never just one person." The myth of singularity must be exposed for the culprit that it is. We learn that by identifying and understanding the various "personalities" within the one personality, we actually feel more together, more sane—even before problems are solved. Bottom line: We all talk to ourselves and we need to get better at it.

2. ASKING "WHO IS IN CHARGE?" Once our multiple nature is clarified, the next logical step is determining who is in charge. (Take me to your leader.) Most of us will discover a powerful little character that I call The Should Monster is at the helm, directing our lives with intimidating

36

should's, ought's and if only's. Here we can begin to see that the distribution of power within our committee is grossly out of whack.

3.   CREATING A DECISION MAKER. Now that we are a crowded conference room ruled by a relentless tyrant, our distress may make more sense—although we may feel worse. But where is the hero of our story? By heightening our awareness of who we are not (The Should Monster in particular) we begin to discover more of who we are, and subsequently what we need in order to emerge as in charge of our own lives: A Decision Maker who can listen to the committee-within and make decisions based on the information available, rather than a policy of perpetual self-indictment.

4.   EMPOWERING THE DECISION MAKER. As difficult as it is to face our own destructive self-criticism, for most of us the greater challenge is in creating and empowering a new leader. We cannot "just say no" without investing in an alternative. And like it or not, that alternative is to do whatever it takes to become powerful, self-caring adults, Decision Makers in charge of our own lives. To be in charge does not mean that we control everything; it simply means that we accept the responsibility of learning how to be the very best adults in our own lives. (A frightening prospect for many of us.)

5.   ESTABLISHING A DAILY PRACTICE. None of this will work until we can accept this simple truth: Perfection is not one of our choices. Practice makes...practice. As long as we insist on striving for the impossible, we will remain the loyal subjects to our Should Monsters. Only through learning to accept—and even to value—our imperfection (otherwise known as being human), will we discover the freedom to enjoy this constant learning experience called life.

In a Nutshell

Let go of your desire for perfection;
embrace you need for flexibility.

28

There is an important difference between two kinds of guilt.

Self-forgiveness is not about abdicating responsibility. If we let ourselves off the hook for things we need to be held responsible for, then self-forgiveness loses all credibility. On the other hand, if we hold ourselves responsible for things that are beyond our control, or if we won't let go of the guilt once we have learned the lessons, we will become less, not more, effective in leading a responsible life.

There are two kinds of guilt: natural and neurotic. Or think of them as rational and irrational. Whatever we call them, one kind of guilt works for us, and the other works against us.

Natural (or rational) guilt is really nothing more than a healthy conscience. It provides motivation for us to correct our course when we fail to behave congruently with our personal value system. In other words, natural guilt occurs when we violate our own, not someone else's, value system. Natural guilt is like a hero from the old western movies: once the job is done, the hero rides off into the sunset. Correction made; guilt gone. (Who was that masked man?)

Neurotic (or irrational) guilt, on the other hand, does not ride off into the sunset. Once this kind of guilt is activated (whether rationally or irrationally), it continues to haunt us, quickly becoming more of a pervasive shame than mere guilt. With neurotic guilt, I might apologize to you and you accept my apology, and I still walk away feeling very badly about myself—experiencing a shame that is directed more toward who I am as a person than at any particular mistake made.

Practice making the distinction between these two kinds of guilt. Pay close attention to the one (natural guilt), and tell the other (neurotic guilt) to…go have a seat at the back of the room. As with most personal growth work, this is far easier said than done, but well worth the effort.

29

Explore and define your
personal value system;
then put it into action.

W hat matters most to you? What are the regrets you definitely don't want to have when you reflect on your life from your deathbed? What are the memories you definitely do want to have as you look back? Are you living this very day of your life in a way that is congruent with your answers to these three questions?

We need to ask ourselves questions like these, and we need to answer them, on a regular basis. It should be like checking the oil in our cars. (I don't remember to do that one either.)

We all have our own unique set of values. It is important that we not assume that we all share the same values, and it is important that we not assume that a value system is fixed. Sure, there will be a number of "standard values" that most of us (hopefully) will share in common, but I am talking about a more subjective, personal value system. These values will vary greatly from one person to another, and will be constantly changing across time. The personal value systems of a 20 year old, and a 40 year old will quite naturally be different.

It is important that we be proactive in exploring and defining our personal value systems, and that we accept responsibility to act in congruence with our values on a daily basis. Too often, we have perfectly good value systems gathering dust in the corner because we are not doing what it takes to put them to good use. And most of us have become a little too proficient at making excuses for not putting our value system into action.

So, today—check your oil and ask yourself these four questions:

1. What matters most to me?

2. What are the regrets I definitely don't want to have when I reflect on my life from my deathbed?

3. What are the memories I definitely do want to have as I look back?

4. Am I living this very day in a way that is congruent with my answers to these three questions?

30

Even negativity has positive applications.

✦

(Part 1)

For years I have emphasized to clients, readers and audiences that we do not have to get rid of the negative messages and toxic beliefs that so effectively haunt our emotions, and sabotage our actions. In fact, one of the ways that we tend to keep ourselves stuck in old patterns of thinking and behaving is believing that we SHOULD be able to expel negativity, and replace it with positive, healthy thinking. When that is what we think, we are once again expecting the impossible of ourselves. And that, of course, becomes one more toxic belief.

One way to think more realistically about overcoming the tyranny of negative beliefs, is to consider how we might put the negativity to some productive use. ("You're already here, and I don't know how to get rid of you, so you might as well lend a hand.") Here is one positive application for your negativity. I will share another one with you next week.

The Positive Application
of Negative Visualization

The next time you are facing something in your life that scares you, rather than fighting the negative predictions from your inner-cynic, go ahead and visualize the worst case scenario. See it in detail, don't hold back. Move right toward the negativity. Your inner-cynic is trying to scare you by asking "What if…" and you are going to call his bluff and answer the question. OK, you say, let's think about "what if…"

Visualize the negative scene in detail, as I said, but here is the key: work with the visualization until you see yourself in the scene responding with confidence and strength. See and feel yourself dealing with the negative situation in a way that will make you proud.

Repeat the visualization (with the strong, confident version of you) several times. Then, imagine that you can package the visualization, and put it away. Put it somewhere where you can easily find it if you need to. Now, invest all of your energy into creating visualizations of various positive outcomes. Practice the positive visualizations like there is no tomorrow.

Expect a positive outcome. You will be able to do this more easily now because you are in far less danger of being distracted by the prophecy of a negative outcome. When your inner-cynic (Should Monster, Threat Monster, whoever it is) shows up with his negative "what if," you look him straight in the eye and say, "I have already answered that question. In fact, I already have a complete plan ready to go in the event of a negative outcome. Now, if you will excuse me, I have better things to do than stand around listening to your crap."

Give it a try. Even let yourself have some fun with it. And let me know what you think.

In a Nutshell

Always move toward your demons.
They take their power
from your retreat.

31

Even negativity has positive applications.

✦

(Part 2)

In last week's E-Minder, I suggested that as long as negativity is going to be hanging around, taking up valuable space in our minds, we might as well put that negativity to some productive use. So last week, I described one way to do that: "The Positive Application of Negative Visualization."

Here is another way to put negativity to work for us.

The Springboard Technique

Choose two or three old, negative beliefs about yourself. Choose beliefs that you would really like to change. Corresponding to each old belief, write a concise new positive belief, a belief that you would prefer. You don't have to believe the new belief; the only requirement is that you want to believe it.

Here are some examples of negative beliefs and corresponding positive beliefs:

Neg: I am destined to move from one crappy relationship to another.

Pos: I am in charge of my choices. It will take some serious work, but I know I can learn to be a healthy person in a healthy relationship.

◆   ◆   ◆

Neg: Life is a no win proposition, so I might as well give up.

Pos: I don't have to perpetuate my family's negative point of view. I will do what it takes to succeed.

◆   ◆   ◆

Neg: Everything goes wrong for me. I am a loser from birth.

Pos: I will find the positive lessons for me to learn, even in the midst of negative situations. I am a winner by choice.

(Write your beliefs in whatever way they occur to you. If these examples are helpful, that's great, but don't "believe" that you have to write yours like the examples.)

Now pick one of your old beliefs to work with for the next week. (This technique works best as you begin when you focus on one belief at a time.) The Springboard technique is quite simple: Memorize the new, positive belief that corresponds to your old negative one. Memorize it verbatim; repeat it over and over until you can say it without even thinking about it. Again, you don't have to believe it. At this point, just memorize it.

For the next week, every time you become aware of the old negative belief, use that awareness to cue a rehearsal of your brand new belief. Every time you are aware of the negative thought, mentally (and when possible, verbally) repeat the new belief multiple times. In other words, you are putting the negative belief to work for you by having it remind you of the need to rehearse your new thinking. You are using the negative as a "springboard" to the positive. Ironically, the more aware you become of your negative thinking over the next week, the more time you will spend thinking positively. Boing!!

Mastering the springboard technique will take some practice, but it is well worth the effort—especially when you consider how wonderfully sneaky it is to actually use the negative thoughts to help you learn positive ones.

<u>In a Nutshell</u>

Since we don't know how to
"exorcise" the negative beliefs,
we might as well
"exercise" the positive ones.

32

Give yourself permission to doubt.

♦

(Permission for the 3-D's, Part 1)

Several years ago, a client who was stuck in some very limiting and abusive religious beliefs and I came up with what we called "Permission for the 3-D's," We developed this idea as a tool to help release her from a belief system that had been handed down, unquestioned and unchanged, through several generations of her family. Since then, I have recognized that "Permission for the 3-D's" is an effective and powerful tool to be used to help any of us remain open-minded, independent thinkers, regardless of the subject matter.

Try putting "Permission for the 3-D's" to work in your life. For the next three weeks, E-Minders will explore these 3-D's. This week, the first of these: PERMISSION TO DOUBT.

It is amazing how frequently we can catch ourselves accepting things at face value, or in the case of limiting or negative beliefs about ourselves, believing things that simply are not true. It can be scary, but the next time you are aware of a negative opinion you have about yourself, take the time to consider the possibility that you may be wrong, that the original source of your belief may have been wrong.

When a client is very attached to a particular negative opinion of herself, I challenge her to put the attorney-within to work establishing "reasonable doubt." Doubt is the first step toward insuring that the beliefs that you have about yourself and the world around you are actually your beliefs. You don't have to instantly disagree with your negative thoughts. Begin with some healthy doubt.

<u>In a Nutshell</u>

Ask yourself,
"How much of what I believe
do I really believe?"

33

Give yourself permission to disagree.

✦

(Permission for the 3'D's, Part2)

Several years ago, a client who was stuck in some very limiting and abusive religious beliefs and I came up with what we called "Permission for the 3-D's," We developed this idea as a tool to help release her from a belief system that had been handed down, unquestioned and unchanged, through several generations of her family. Since then, I have recognized that "Permission for the 3-D's" is an effective and powerful tool to be used to help any of us remain open-minded, independent thinkers, regardless of the subject matter.

With last week's E-Minder, we identified the first of the 3-D's: permission to doubt. This week, let's look at the second D: PERMISSION TO DISAGREE.

It is important to think about who the "share holders" in your self-image are. Who gets to decide what the truth about you is? Too often, we have grown up automatically granting tremendous credibility to people who will predictably have a negative view of us. When our self-esteem is low, people who have such negative views will have credibility, while someone who thinks well of us is in danger of losing all credibility. "If you like me, and especially if you respect me," we think, "then you clearly don't know what you are talking about." This is reminiscent of the famous Groucho Marx line: "I wouldn't be a member of any club that would have me."

Thinking negatively about ourselves is, among other things, a very bad habit. If you are serious about personal growth, you will need to make a commitment to yourself to carefully consider perceptions and beliefs about you—yours and others'—and make a conscious decision about whether or not you agree with each perception and belief. (Note: it is not unusual to discover at first that you agree with most negative thoughts about yourself. Keep shining the light of awareness on them, and keep sharing them with others you trust, and I promise that you will learn to disagree.)

Once you have given yourself permission to doubt the truth of what others may say or think about you, and even to doubt your own habitual beliefs about yourself, it is imperative that you follow up by giving yourself permission to disagree with the same. Frequently, after a hear a client express a negative opinion about him or herself—an opinion that I know is part of a bad habit of negative thinking—I will ask, "Yeah, but what do you think?"

Try this: the next time you are aware of a negative thought about yourself, stop and ask the question they ask contestants on The Hollywood Squares: "Agree or disagree?"

34

Give yourself permission to decide.

✦

(Permission for the 3'D's, Part2)

Several years ago, a client who was stuck in some very limiting and abusive religious beliefs and I came up with what we called "Permission for the 3-D's," We developed this idea as a tool to help release her from a belief system that had been handed down, unquestioned and unchanged, through several generations of her family. Since then, I have recognized that "Permission for the 3-D's" is an effective and powerful tool to be used to help any of us remain open-minded, independent thinkers, regardless of the subject matter.

In the last two E-Minders, we identified the first two of the 3-D's: permission to doubt, and permission to disagree. This week, let's look at the third (and final) D: PERMISSION TO DECIDE.

The permission to decide is the corner stone of self-respect. Giving ourselves permission—and holding ourselves responsible—to consciously and thoughtfully decide for ourselves what we believe is how we distinguish ourselves as individual, adult human beings. Unfortunately, when we have been discouraged from even expressing doubt about beliefs and value systems that have been passed down from one generation to another, we can find ourselves a long way from being the primary decision makers in our own lives. Religious belief systems that view humanity as fundamentally bad, and black &white political beliefs are good examples of this. When religious doctrine is drilled into us to "save us from ourselves," we are hardly encouraged to have confidence in ourselves as decision-makers. When we are taught to distrust a person solely based on his or her political affiliation, we are not being decision-makers at all.

Make a list of beliefs and values that you have received from your family, your school, your church, etc, as you have grown up. Often these beliefs are so much a part of us, we need to make such a list over a period of a few days, giving ourselves enough opportunity to become aware of them. These may be beliefs about the world we live in, beliefs about particular people or groups of people, or specific beliefs about you. Consider each of the beliefs on your list in terms of the 3-D's. Give yourself permission to question, and express doubt. Give yourself permission to disagree if that is your inclination. And whether you agree or disagree, be sure that you make your own decision.

And keep giving yourself permission for the 3-D's, even when others around you object.

In a Nutshell

Making a mistake does not
make you a mistake.

35

There is such a thing as healthy apathy.

Apathy can be a dangerous thing. It has played a very big role in my life, as a psychological defense. e.g. "If I just don't give a sh—, then I am less likely to be affected (aka: hurt) by what is happening in my life." In this way, apathy has not only helped me to stuff lots of feelings into the basement of my consciousness, but it has also kept me from taking important risks that would have facilitated at least more psychological growth, and possibly more personal and professional success. That kind of apathy I don't need. And when I hear it talking to me (he is The Cynic on my committee), I am wise to pay attention and identify and express what I am really feeling. Usually, the best question to ask myself here is "What am I afraid of?"

But sometimes we just think too much. One of the side effects of personal growth work is that we become so skilled at analyzing and understanding ourselves and others around us, that we just keep going and going—like that Energizer Bunny. When this is going on, a little apathy can be a very useful thing. "Why don't we just let it go," I tell myself. "It's just not that important to figure it out."

Learn to differentiate between apathy as a psychological defense, and apathy as an excellent idea. The only way to do this—as with most personal growth work—is to practice. In this case, practice identifying examples of both kinds of apathy in your thinking. When is "not caring much" a way for you to avoid something important, but potentially unpleasant, and when is "not caring much" an effective way of not sweating the small stuff?

<u>In a Nutshell</u>

Forget about finding
the right answers.
Just make a list of
some very good questions.

36

There are two major "food groups" (sources) for self-esteem.

The two major food groups (sources) of self-esteem are DOING and BEING. We need to be nourished from both sources in a more or less balanced way. Most of us experience, to one degree or another, an imbalance, weighted toward excessive reliance on the DOING-ESTEEM, with a deficit in BEING-ESTEEM.

The self-esteem we gain from DOING is the conditional regard we have for ourselves. In this arena, we define ourselves according to our performance in the various roles of life. i.e. worker, spouse, parent, church member, friend, etc. It is here that our healthy conscience operates, steering us along a relatively virtuous path by providing natural guilt signals to which we can respond in order to correct our course.

Also in DOING-ESTEEM, we experience motivation to set goals, to accomplish those goals, and even to master certain functions in our lives—learning over time to be the best widget maker, parent, spouse, etc. that we can be. Here we evaluate ourselves according to outcome and accomplishment, but [in the person with strong self-esteem] we also credit ourselves for positive intention and for our efforts. By evaluating ourselves according to intention and effort in addition to outcome, we never have to lose too much ground when we fall short of a goal. We can be disappointed without being devastated.

DOING-ESTEEM works best when it is supported by a healthy amount of BEING-ESTEEM. In this way, even when our efforts fall short or fail, we still experience ourselves as essentially good, well meaning people. Without the foundation of BEING-ESTEEM, when we fall short in our DOING efforts, our self-esteem is in danger of total collapse. "I have failed in my attempt to do such and such," becomes "I am a failure," a global negative self-judgment far beyond the scope of what we are capable of doing or not doing.

BEING-ESTEEM is an unconditional self-acceptance. This positive regard is not dependent on our abilities to function well in any particular role. The BEING-ESTEEM is a birth right really; it is best characterized as the feeling we experience toward an infant, newly arrived on the planet. The infant is not required to do anything in order to procure full unconditional acceptance.

When the two sources of self-esteem coexist, we have a base line sense of our natural goodness, of our benevolence, with no felt need to earn self-acceptance for who we are. With the BEING-ESTEEM solidly in place, we are in an excellent position to risk new behaviors, and even to try on new ways of defining ourselves, just as toddlers beginning to explore their world, feeling the security of their parents' love and protection, are inclined to take risks in their explorations. The very positive consequence of this combination of the two sources of self-esteem—for toddlers and adults alike—is an increased likelihood of mastery in the world of DOING. It is interesting to consider the interaction between the two sources: our capabilities as Do-er's will be significantly enhanced by a strong positive regard for ourselves as Beings, but the reverse is not true. No matter how hard we try, we cannot strengthen unconditional positive regard for ourselves by DOING more, or DOING better.

In a Nutshell

You can do great things,
and never come close to perfect.

37

Gratitude can be used as a defense.

Have you ever listened to someone else's plight, or even just watched a homeless person cross the street, and thought, "What right do I have to complain about anything?" It is important to see our lives in proper perspective, and comparing our circumstances with others less fortunate, or with bigger problems, can be useful in helping us to keep that perspective. It's simple gratitude, and it is an essential ingredient to the fully responsible life.

But gratitude can also be used to help us avoid taking responsibility for ourselves. If I am upset about something in my life, something that needs my attention, I might say "Well, I don't have it as bad as Bob," or "At least I have my health and a roof over my head." I can say these things to express genuine gratitude, but I might say the same things to support my tendency to avoid taking action needed to solve my problem. In the case of the latter, I am misusing gratitude to avoid taking responsibility for myself. The difference between the two meanings may be subtle, but it is important that we learn to make that distinction if we are serious about living a fully responsible life.

We can also misuse gratitude by using it as a weapon against ourselves. We say, "How dare I express any dissatisfaction when others have worse problems than mine." This does not help us regain the proper perspective of genuine gratitude. It helps us avoid taking action, and attacks our self-esteem in the process. Very efficient, huh?

What we must keep in mind if we are to avoid misusing gratitude in these ways is that gratitude and dissatisfaction can (and often do) co-exist. Expressing dissatisfaction does not necessarily mean we are ungrateful for what we have.

38

Blame and responsibility are not the same thing.

When something goes wrong, are you more likely to blame yourself or someone else? The question is important for a couple of different reasons.

First, your honest answer will indicate if you are better described as a "perfectionist" or an "excuser." And second, the question itself brings us face to face with the need to differentiate between blame and responsibility.

Are you a perfectionist or an excuser? Most of us have characteristics of both, but we tend to lean in one direction or another, like being left or right handed. Perfectionists are relentlessly self-critical, usually much tougher on themselves than on anyone else—practicing that "dangerous double standard." Excusers are very creative about letting themselves off the hook, perceiving problems as someone else's fault, or blaming what's wrong on the circumstances themselves.

To me, the most interesting part of this thinking about Perfectionists and Excusers, is that both tendencies are ways of avoiding responsibility.

Perfectionists and Excusers alike tend to see themselves as responsible people, but both approaches waste valuable energy that could be better used for effectively resolving problems. The only real difference between the two are "how" we create the energy leaks. Energy channeled into beating myself up is just as wasted as energy I use to blame someone else for my problems.

The key to plugging these "energy leaks" is discovered when we learn to let go of our defensive need to place blame for what has already happened, focusing our attention instead on what we can learn from past mistakes, and what we can do differently—starting right now.

I admit that there is nothing original in this message, but there is a big difference between "knowing something" and "doing something." I have learned that a big part of my job is to keep reminding people (myself included) of what we already know, and providing encouragement to put that knowledge into action.

So whether you are a Perfectionist or an Excuser, the real question is, "What are you going to do about it?"

<u>In a Nutshell</u>

Learn from failure and
it becomes success.

39

Be your own lead sled dog.

Imagine you are one of a team of six big, strong huskies harnessed in single file to a sled full of provisions for the winter. Now, imagine that you are the lead dog. Now, imagine that you (the lead dog) are lying down, unable or unwilling to stand up and pull the sled.

How successful will the other five dogs on the team be in pulling the sled as long as you are lying down?

This is one of my favorite metaphors. It is just so simple and clear.

Each of us is our own lead sled dog. No matter how much potential exists in the friends and family who love and support us, their potential is useless until we stand up and start pulling. The moment we accept our responsibility as lead sled dog, and "mush" forward, we harness our own strength and the strength of all the other dogs to help us plow ahead.

When I think of my life in these terms, I can really feel the power and support backing me up.

A MEMO to my former suicidal self:

"Our limitations are never greater than our potential to overcome them."

Is this true? Maybe, maybe not. Either way, I choose to live according to this belief because I despise the alternative—which is to accept victimization, and ultimately to give up.

If believing this is delusional and naïve, that's OK with me. I would rather die delusional, naïve, and still trying than give up.

In a Nutshell

Everything is a phase

40

Challenge your low self-esteem and surprise yourself. (I did.)

None of us needs help telling ourselves that we should change our behavior if we want to feel better. Our constant companion, The Should Monster, covers that ground with great competence. What we do need help with is getting on our own side, learning to support ourselves toward the changes that we desire, as opposed to the highly ineffective means of attempting to shame ourselves into change.

I had a therapist many years ago who challenged me to make a list of all the accomplishments in my life that I attribute to "shoulding" (shaming) myself. I left that session confident that I would produce a substantial list for our next session, thereby proving to my therapist that she didn't know what she was talking about. (I wonder why we work so hard to prove to our therapists that they are idiots. Are we really that attached to the negative views we have of ourselves?)

Much to my surprise, and later to my pleasure, I couldn't come up with anything for my list. Oh sure, I had pushed and shoved myself into doing a lot of things because I "should," but when it came right down to it I couldn't call these "successes via shaming" because in the end, no matter what I had "accomplished," I still felt like crap about myself. And I had been in therapy long enough to know that something that leaves me feeling like crap is probably not an accomplishment. I was no idiot. (Remember, it was my hypothesis that my therapist was the idiot.)

As it turned out, she wasn't. And the big surprise: neither was I. Even though I could go around saying, "I'm no idiot," inside I had pretty much accepted my idiocy as a fact of life—my life.

Somehow my therapist's challenging therapy assignment shook something loose in me; I became unstuck. It was like I dropped the low self-esteem ball that I had been gripping with all my strength (a death-grip, pun intended). In a strange way, she had tricked me—tricked me into seeing my true idiocy: believing that somehow the way I had always been doing things was going to work…someday. Someday, somehow I would shame and slap myself from just the right angle and abracadabra, I'd be a changed man.

Since I wasn't an idiot (or at least was determined to become a recovering idiot), with an excellent therapist's help, I began to take self-compassion lessons.

I now know that to learn something new we must first acknowledge what we "don't know." And then (here comes the tough part): we must accept the responsibility to do whatever it takes to abstain from the old, toxic behaviors and beliefs. By doing the hard work of clearing out the old we may experience tremendous fear, confusion and aimless wandering, but we will finally be making room for something new. In this case, something new and radical like treating ourselves with the same kindness and generosity that we have for others.

41

Questions make excellent tools.

W e are all familiar with "the power of positive thinking"—i.e.

- I am a loveable, deserving child of God.

- I deserve that new job.

- I am capable and willing to do what it takes to be in a healthy relationship.

  —and the application of practical wisdom to our daily lives. i.e.

- Practice conversations 'to convey' rather than 'to convince'.

- Making mistakes does not make you a mistake.

- Respect is not necessarily expressed through agreement.

Positive affirmation and practical wisdom are important tools in the construction and maintenance of our personal growth. But in our impatience for answers, it is easy to overlook another kind of tool that is handy to keep around: Questions.

Here are a few questions to consider. Let them work like magnets, attracting not just one quick answer, but many thoughts and ideas. These are questions to contemplate.

- How much of what you believe do you really believe?

- Can you tell when you are using your intelligence to avoid learning?

- What if the more afraid we became, the more faith would automatically kick in?

- Are you solving the problems you want to solve, or the problems you think you are "supposed" to solve?

- What is the difference between making excuses and practicing self-compassion?

- Two questions: When is the last time you left your house without getting dressed? When is the last time you left your house without making a conscious contact with God?

- How would today be different if you could replace your "desire for perfection" with the awareness of your "need for flexibility?"

- If life is an essay test, what question are you working on now?

- What is the difference between boredom and being at peace?

  A couple more questions to consider…

- Suppose we discover that the purpose for human existence is for each of us to fully experience embarrassment. How would you be doing so far?

- Is the opposite of forgive and forget…resent and remember?

42

Recovery goes both ways.

I am a recovering alcoholic. I have also wrestled with depression for most of my life. Today, thanks to lots of good psychotherapy and a state-of-the-art (or science) medication, I am also recovering from depression. The irony is not lost on me: if I put alcohol or other mood-altering chemicals into my body, my life will quickly spiral out of control; and if I do not put a certain anti-depressant chemical into my body, my life will quickly spiral out of control.

Like many others I have known, I have gone through the anger at the "horrible injustice" of my having alcoholism and depression. Why me? Why can other people have a drink at the end of the day and I can't? And why do I have to remember to take this damn little pill twice a day, while I watch others move through their lives with an apparent consistent flow of energy, in relatively good moods?

And so I ask God, "Why me?"

I can never be completely sure about which of the myriad of voices inside my crowded head is speaking, but if I am not mistaken, God has answered.

"Why not you?" God said.

What's interesting about this thing I call my recovery is that I no longer object to having alcoholism or depression. I did my share of complaining through college and graduate school about the work that I did not want to do, but there was never a time when I did not understand that school was a means to an end. In the bigger picture of my life, I see alcoholism and depression in that same light. And I have become grateful for the path I have traveled. School is not always easy—especially the really good schools—but the lessons I have learned are, without question, worth the difficulties I have encountered along the way.

That doesn't mean that I don't have regrets, that if I had it to do over again, I wouldn't change a thing. But it does mean that I understand that facing and dealing with those regrets has been, and will continue to be, a significant part of my education.

One of the most helpful concepts about recovery happens to be one of the most simple: when I stop fighting for my right to deny the obvious (that I have alcoholism and depression), I am free to begin the exploration of who I really am, and who I really want to be. I think of it as using the word "recovery" in two different directions: I must do whatever it takes to "recover from" what is destructive or toxic to me, so that I can recover (meaning "regain") the genuine me.

It's my life's work.

In a Nutshell

As an addict, I must learn to
quit while I'm behind.
Only then can I get ahead.

43

Living in the moment is like riding a unicycle.

Have you ever attempted to ride a unicycle? Well, it ain't easy. But as with so many skills, those who can ride a unicycle certainly make it look easy. Maybe this is because once the skill is learned, it is performed "with ease," even though it was not easy to learn.

The same is true of the skill called "living-in-the-moment." Present-tense living requires the same balance, the same focus and the same relaxed awareness as riding a unicycle. Leaning too far backward (living in the past) or too far forward (living in the future) will always result in your falling off.

Being centered on the unicycle and holding a focus on where you are going will get you there. And as long as you hold your balance, you can always change directions.

When you are riding a unicycle, or when you are living-in-the-moment, you will be doing it with ease. There is no other way. This feeling of "ease" is how you know you are performing the skill. Tension will throw you off balance.

Important note: In learning to ride a unicycle, one becomes willing to fall, even to accept bumps, bruises and scrapes. And one remains committed to standing back up, picking up the unicycle and getting back on. That's what it takes.

Happy cycling!

A LITTLE MORE ABOUT BALANCE: Balance and perfection are entirely different. When you strive for perfection, expect disappointment and self-resentment. When you strive for balance, just expect to be busy—because it is a lifelong job.

<u>In a Nutshell</u>

Courage is to fear as
light is to darkness.

44

Don't be surprised by the predictable.

Denial's job is to keep us in the dark. We cannot resolve what we cannot identify. In our efforts to shine light into that darkness—to do what we can to reveal the truth so we can deal with the truth—denial hangs on with a death grip. Pun intended.

One of denial's clever, most stubborn, strategies is "surprise." Here are a couple of examples:

"Can you believe Bob said that to me?!" I say this with outrage, even though Bob has been saying things like that to me for as long as I have known him.

or

"Can you believe she would do something like that?!" I ask the rhetorical question even though she has been doing "things like that" for the past 10 years.

When we repeatedly ask these questions—of ourselves or others—about people who have consistently done or said what seemingly baffles us, we are not experiencing genuine surprise; this is denial at work.

If someone has consistently treated you badly, if a situation has consistently yielded negative results, and you have made reasonable (or beyond reasonable) efforts to change the outcome…it is time to stop being surprised. Sometimes the answer to the question, "Can you believe that?!" is simply, "Yes, I believe it."

Shine a little more light into the dark corners where denial still hides. Stop being surprised by the predictable.

In a Nutshell

Don't let your insights
live with you rent-free.
Put them to work.

45

Anybody can have a good day on a good day.

It is amazing how often we mistake the sense of familiarity for safety. When times are tough, it is very easy to slide back into old, dysfunctional behaviors, and then dig ourselves in a little deeper by bowing down once again to our old friend and inner-tyrant, The Should Monster. Self-criticism and shame are no doubt legitimate problems, but as we make our way along roads less traveled, the same self-criticism and shame may become excellent hideouts, refuges from the often difficult work of personal growth and recovery.

Beware of lingering tendencies of self-blame and condemnation in the face of personal challenge. Expect that when the going gets tough, the Should Monster will welcome you back with open arms, happy to have you safe and sound, and home again. Don't get too comfortable there, no matter how familiar (perceived as safe) it may feel.

To counter this backsliding tendency, use these three checkpoints:

1. <u>Practice Self-Compassion.</u> This is not to be mistaken for letting yourself off the hook. Accepting responsibility for ourselves is at the very core of genuine personal growth. But don't waste valuable time and energy beating yourself up for beating yourself up. We have all spent many years rehearsing dysfunctional and toxic ways of thinking and behaving. Don't expect to successfully change without a great deal of dedicated practice. And even then, expect imperfection—it is the nature of the human condition.

2. <u>Take a Breather.</u> This is very often the most difficult thing to do, but it is important to learn how to take a break. You must directly rebel against the perfectionist-within, and do the previously unthinkable: lower your expectations. After sliding back into old behaviors, you may just need to stop and catch your breath. So breathe—that's why they call it a breather.

3. <u>Brush Yourself Off and Get Back in There.</u> Getting stuck in self-criticism is not an effective means of taking responsibility. Neither accept responsibility for what is outside of your control, nor hide from responsibility for that which you can control. (That's right: the good ole Serenity Prayer) There is an old Chinese proverb that says it quite simply: "Fall down sixteen times, get up seventeen."

The bottom line is that anybody can have a good day on a good day. The measure of our personal progress comes on the not-so-good days.

In a Nutshell

Self-blame is not responsibility.

46

Recognize the value of these are uncertain times.

In no uncertain terms: life is uncertain. Haven't you noticed?

Just when it all seems to be settling in around us, just when we begin to trust the constancy, the predictability of our day to day lives, WHAM! Something new, and possibly not so improved puts its foot on the edge of our boat, and rocks it. And still, so many of us live with our don't-rock-the-boat philosophy, darting from hiding place to hiding place in hopes that finally we will be able to avoid the dreaded nature of life: UNCERTAINTY.

That's right: the nature of life. Uncertainty is not some renegade spoiler plotting to interfere with the pleasant (and consistent) plans we have for ourselves. Uncertainty is not the foe that we must defeat in order to live happily ever after. Uncertainty is not the Darth Vader to our Luke Skywalker.

Uncertainty is a very ingenious means to the all important end.

Think about it. What makes the difference between the successful and the unsuccessful, the purposeful and the aimless, the happy and the miserable? It is our relationship with uncertainty that will determine all of this—and (as they say in the advertising business) much, much more!

If I decide that I am out of shape, aging a little less than gracefully, and if I decide to respond to my awareness by acknowledging the need to get into better shape and begin going to the gym three times a week, I am not going to be surprised and offended at the exercise that awaits me at the gym. Well, maybe I will. But if I am, I will certainly be missing the point. And if I remain surprised, offended or resistant in any of the multitude of other ways at which I am so adept, I can be sure that the flab that I detest will not be transforming into the muscle that I long for.

Consider this: What if human life is the gym, and uncertainty is the exercise? What if we are aging, increasingly flabby souls in a universe that reaches far beyond this little health club we call earth? What if we have come here, every one of us, to get into better shape? Picture it. A crowded little gym with a bunch of out of shape souls running around (I suppose there is some aerobic value there) avoiding exercise.

Uncertainty is exercise for the soul? An ingenious means to an all important end?

Yep. At least I think so. Through our relationship with all that is uncertain in this sometimes smelly gym called earth, we are constantly challenged to remember what is really important to us. Daily—or at least three time per week—we are faced with the opportunity to "work out" our personal value systems. Our distractibility, our tendency to lose our place, is the flab of our souls. Our genuine value system (not just expressed, but lived) is the muscle.

In these uncertain times, I think it's as good a guess as any. Of course, I can't be sure.

47

Lots of things change; truth remains simple.

I was facilitating self-compassion workshops long before I wrote my first book. Once, a workshop participant told me that what I was doing couldn't really be considered a "workshop" unless I offered a "handout." In response to her comment I developed a handout, Six Simple Truths, that became the impetus for my first book. Twelve years later, I am in the process of finishing what will be my sixth book—and I frequently still use that handout. For our purposes we can call the handout Six Simple E-minders. Here they are:

SIX SIMPLE TRUTHS
For a Vital Self-Image

1. <u>I Create My Own Reality.</u> The key word in this much over worked phrase is "create." From what I have been handed, I creatively build a reality for myself. "I create my own reality" is not another way to say that I am to blame for this whole mess, but instead that I have the power to do something with it. (These days, I tend to think of this one as "I am in charge of my life even when I am not in control." No matter what we call it, it is about accepting personal responsibility.)

2. <u>I Feel What I Feel.</u> Once I recognize a feeling (emotion) within me, my only choice is about how I will express that feeling. Laborious attempts to talk myself out of, or in any way to try to change or deny the feeling will simply drain me of energy that might be more effectively used elsewhere.

3. <u>My One Self Contains Many Selves.</u> We are all on a path of integration. Before I can become "one," I must make peace with the many. Making peace does not necessarily mean agreeing with or over-identifying with any one of

my "parts." It simply means that I respect those "parts" as real and valid—that I give myself permission to have more than one opinion and more than one feeling about things.

4. <u>My Emotional-Self and My Thinking-Self Are Intended for a 50/50 Partnership</u>. An important human task is to bring this mind/heart relationship into balance, letting go of the need for one having to dominate the other. For most of us, this is a lifetime of work.

5. <u>I Am Here To Learn.</u> I think of my earth life as an education. With this belief I am finally free to be the perfectly imperfect human being (student) that I am. I no longer have to remain stuck in all-or-none, right-or-wrong, good-or-bad thinking. Now I can judge myself according to my intentions and my efforts—and just keep learning.

6. <u>Self Love Is True Love</u>. I realize now that love and sacrifice are not the same; and that the most effective way to give the gift of love to others is to accept it first for myself. I remember that there is an important distinction between "selfishness" and taking excellent care of myself.

48

Start change with some good questions.

If you are interested in changing something about yourself, start with a few questions—

1. Do I really want to make this change?

    Don't assume that the only answer to this question is yes. Remember that our minds are crowded with those pesky little committee members. Listen to all sides of the argument. Motivation to make the change does not have to be unanimous among the committee members, but we set ourselves up for failure when we proceed to the next questions without a strong desire to make the change. Spend as much time as you need on this question.

2. Do I have a history of success with making this kind of change?

    One common mistake is failing to remember and return to what has proven successful in the past. Our impatient, hyper-active minds seem to always want to come up with some new approach. Of course one reason for this is our never-ending search for the "effortless way." (I'm thinking of writing a book called "Buy This Book and Be Healed," with the subtitle being, "You Don't Even Have to Read It.")

3. If I have attempted this change previously, specifically how have I failed?

    It is difficult to review the film of a losing game, but every football team does it. We tend to react to failure with one extreme or the other: we try to act like nothing happened at all, or we ruthlessly beat ourselves up for falling short. Neither of these approaches is productive. Accurate and objective information gathered by evaluating failed attempts to change will help us in answering the next question.

4. <u>If I have failed previously, what will make this time different from the last?</u>

    When we neither ignore our failed attempts to change (hoping they will go away), nor beat ourselves senseless for being imperfect humans, we are in a position to make a plan. Answering this question thoroughly will result in a specific plan for accomplishing the goal set.

49

A decision is an excellent place to start, but it's only a start.

Even the strongest decision to change is not enough to get the job done. A few months ago, I came to the decision that I wanted to learn how to play the harmonica (God knows why). My decision was—and still is—real; I do want to learn to play the harmonica. But these many months after making my decision, I have not even touched a harmonica; and if you handed me one, I would not be able to make music with it…because my decision has not taught me to play. I am reminded of how many times I decided to quit drinking, only to continue.

We mistakenly believe that when we fall short of achieving a goal, our decision must be lacking in strength. We say, "I must not want it bad enough." This implies that if we want something "bad enough," it will magically—or at least easily—be ours. We fail to recognize that making a solid decision is only the beginning, and if we do not consciously decide how to follow that decision with specific action, the results (aka: the lack of results) are predictable. In other words, a decision cannot teach you to play the harmonica.

A specific plan for change will include certain components: Action, Support, and Success. This is the memorable acronym I told you about in last week's E-Minder: A.S.S. (If I am serious about change, I have to get my A.S.S. in gear.)

Action. I cannot count the number of times in my life (so far) that I have been dissatisfied with something and genuinely wanted change, but did not take the practical steps necessary to bring the desired change to fruition. The necessity for action is exactly this necessary: if you are not taking responsible action to instigate the change you want, don't expect results.

Support. As a recovering alcoholic I have learned something that I believe is a universal human truth: I cannot achieve and maintain my progress entirely on my own. The good news is that I don't have to. Sure there are stretches of the journey that we all must walk solo, but most of the time we will need support. Keep in mind that, contrary to popular opinion, knowing when, how, and to whom to reach for support is strength, not weakness.

Success. Sometimes succeeding at change is the biggest challenge of all. As strange as it sounds, you must become willing to learn how to let yourself succeed. This is done by letting go of perfectionistic beliefs that success comes all at once as a complete package, and establishing a daily practice of giving yourself credit for the "baby steps" in the right direction. Success is built, not instantly created.

50

Wake up!

◆

(For Corinne)

When someone we know dies, we wake up. When someone we know dies suddenly, unexpectedly, we are awakened as if by a loud noise, startled out of a sound sleep. When we are awakened like that, a burst of adrenaline releasing through our bodies a split second after the noise, it takes a minute or two to become oriented. What happened? Where am I? Who am I? Did something happen? Did it happen right here in my house, or was it in my dream?

The older I get the more experience with these awakenings I accumulate. And yes, I am fully aware that the snooze period between alarm-rings only gets shorter from here. But that's OK, because I don't want to go back to sleep. I want to remain wide-awake, fully aware of how precious—and limited—our time on this earth is.

My friend, Corinne Miltiades, died last week. She was not old, and she had not been seriously ill. (This reminds me of the obits that sometimes tell us the person who died had been in perfect health—I don't think so.) Corinne and I were not close friends; we were just two people whose paths crossed many years ago, who liked and respected each other, and who kept in touch sporadically. We have been in touch a little more lately because of the convenience of e-mail.

I know that Corinne was a terrific person: very loving, very smart, very funny, three of my favorite attributes. I know that her family, her close friends, and her clients (she was a top-notch psychotherapist) will have to endure big ole broken hearts. My wife and I will always appreciate Corinne for a trip to Savannah she made possible for us many years ago, a trip that became a very special memory for Dede and me. I can't remember if I ever told Corinne that.

Corinne has died, and those of us within earshot have been awakened, startled out of various depths of sleep. That is the potential good news. I write this to increase the chances that I will fulfill some of that potential, to improve the chances that I won't be falling back to sleep right away. But I will doze back off eventually. It's part of my chronically forgetful human condition. It's that pesky imperfection that makes us all so interesting.

But I won't forget Corinne. I won't forget that she was here and that she made a big difference in many people's lives. I won't forget that she and I liked each other. And in addition to the gratitude for that special Savannah weekend…

Thank you, Corinne, for the wake-up call.

CHECK YOUR SOUL'S PULSE: Do something today to demonstrate that you are alive, that you are more than a circulatory, cognition-generating, breathing machine——Alive!

51

God bless every life that has been so drastically changed by the events of this horrible day. God bless us all. (9-11-01)

I have been sitting here not knowing what I could possibly write as a weekly e-minder. What could it matter. I knew that everyone would understand if there just wasn't one. Then my friend and young writing colleague, Jenni Schaefer, sent me some of her words, with a note saying, "I don't know what I would do with these feelings if I couldn't write."

When I read them I cried because it was exactly what I needed to hear.

I asked Jenni's permission to share them with you, and she graciously agreed.

September 11, 2001

How does one feel when thousands of lives vanish in an instant? How do you feel when the things that only happen in the movies are flashing across your television screen—live? How does one feel when there is nothing you can do but sit and watch? There is a sense of loss and a feeling of extreme sorrow that overcomes you.

On the street, you look into the eyes of strangers, and you know—you just know. You know they feel it too. From New York City, Washington D.C., and Pennsylvania, the dust comes, and rushes into Detroit, Dallas, Shreveport—and the small towns, too. You cannot escape it. You can try. You can leave work, turn off your radios and televisions, go to sleep, but you cannot get away. You breathe it in. Once inside your head, it enters your heart and soul. And you want to help.

You love your neighbor. You love the clerk at the grocery store. You love the boss that you always hated. And the ink stain on your new skirt no longer matters. Your heart is so heavy, and you just pray. Because you know that God is still here. He will reach out his hands to those you want to save. He will give grace to those who never knew what they would do if they lost their son, daughter, father, mother. He will get them through to the other side.

And you, He will help you, too. He will lift the dark cloud and let the light in again. While He rescues everyone, He feels the most grief of all. He knew everyone who died today. He loved them. He created them. And He mourns for them and their families. And He loves us all. And we feel that too.

We will never forget September 11, 2001. But we will get through it. We will live again.

—Jennifer L. Schaefer/9-11-01

52

Peace is built over time, not created in an instant.

On Friday I told a client who is trying to figure out "who she will be "since she is now successfully recovering from at least three primary addictive behaviors (alcohol, food, relationships), that identity is not something we discover as a whole, but rather something we build as we collect the various pieces along the way. Essentially she is beginning her efforts to find peace within herself.

I believe (nothing original here) that the principles of finding peace within the individual are the same principles we need to put into practice to find peace globally, and just as individuals become overwhelmed by such a seemingly enormous task, it is easy for citizens of the world to become overwhelmed, leaving us more vulnerable to defensive, delusional thinking characterized by over-simplifications of what we face today, and how we must act in response.

The short version: we are so uncomfortable with uncertainty that we will opt for a negative certainty over an uncertainty with a longer-term positive potential. I see this every day in my therapy practice. I have experienced it again and again in my personal life. Right now, in our post-Tuesday world, the stakes are extremely high. It has never been more important for each of us to remain wide-awake, alert, and fully conscious that every choice we make contributes to the big ripple effect of humanity.

About the Author

Thom Rutledge has been called "The Most Entertaining Tour Guide Along The Road Less Traveled." A psychotherapist and professional speaker, Mr. Rutledge is the author of several non-fiction books, including *Embracing Fear & Finding the Courage to Live Your Life*. For more information about books and tapes, or to schedule Mr. Rutledge as a speaker for your next event, call (615) 327-3423, e-mail thomrutledge@earthlink.net, or visit his web site http://www.thomrutledge.com.

To Subscribe to Thom's E-minders:
To receive the e-mail feature, "Thom's E-minders (for the therapeutically forgetful)," e-mail thomrutledge@earthlink.net with "subscribe" in the subject line.

To Order Embracing Fear:
http://www.amazon.com/exec/obidos/ASIN/0062517740/qid%3D1012402077/sr%3D2-1/ref%3Dsr%5F2%5F11%5F1/102-0391418-5794533

0-595-28005-6

Made in the USA
Middletown, DE
29 November 2014